Child Care Grant    4/02    $10.00

# SECRETS OF THE UNEXPLAINED

# Spooky Spectres

by Gary L. Blackwood

**BENCHMARK BOOKS**

MARSHALL CAVENDISH
NEW YORK

Benchmark Books
Marshall Cavendish Corporation
99 White Plains Road
Tarrytown, New York 10591

Library of Congress Cataloging-in-Publication Data
Blackwood, Gary L.
Spooky spectres / by Gary L. Blackwood.
p.   cm. — (Secrets of the unexplained)
Includes bibliographical references and index.
Summary: Presents supposed true-life accounts of ghosts in such categories as
"Short-lived Spectres," "Persistent Phantasms," and "Homemade Spooks."
ISBN 0-7614-0746-4
1. Ghosts—Juvenile literature. [1. Ghosts.]
I. Title. II. Series: Blackwood, Gary L. Secrets of the unexplained.
BF1461.B53   1999   133.1—dc21   98-28281   CIP   AC

Photo research by Debbie Needleman
Photo credits
Cover: Courtesy of F. Reginato/The Image Bank; pages 6, 62: Charles Walker Collection/Stock Montage; pages
10–11: Derek Stafford/Fortean Picture Library; pages 12, 21, 28, 36: Fortean Picture Library; page 15: K.F.
Lord/Fortean Picture Library; page 18: Marina Jackson/Fortean Picture Library; page 20: Corbis-Bettmann;
page 24: Steve Huschle/The Image Bank; page 31: Harry Price Collection/Mary Evans Picture Library; pages
32–33: Hulton Getty Images/Liaison International; pages 39, 47, 57, 70: Mary Evans Picture Library; page 42:
UPI/Corbis-Bettmann; pages 43, 44: Adam Hart-Davis/Fortean Picture Library; page 45: Science Photo
Library/Photo Researchers; page 49 (both): Dr. Elmar R. Gruber/Fortean Picture Library; page 51: Ken
Webster/Fortean Picture Library; pages 52–53: Columbia (Courtesy of Kobal); page 59: Society for Psychical
Research/Mary Evans Picture Library; page 64: Peter Underwood/Mary Evans Picture Library; page 66: Richard
Watt/Gamma; page 69: Roger Brown/Fortean Picture Library; page 72: Michel Tcherevkoff/The Image Bank.
Printed in Hong Kong

1   3   5   6   4   2

# Contents

## PART THREE
# Hauntings

# Introduction

 The Marquise du Deffand, an eighteenth-century noblewoman, was once asked if she believed in ghosts. "Oh, no," she replied. "But I am afraid of them."

A lot of us share Mme du Deffand's outlook. Our logical side says that of course there are no ghosts; the whole notion is just primitive superstition.

But when you pass a graveyard or a creepy old house at night, some deeper part of you rises up and overrules the logical part. The back of your neck prickles. A chill goes up your spine. You start seeing things. Your mind throws logic to the wind and begins to say, like the Cowardly Lion in *The Wizard of Oz*, "I do, I do, I *do* believe in spooks!"

It's no wonder we have such mixed feelings. On the one hand, science has taught us to accept only things we can see, and most of us have never actually seen a ghost. In fact, according to a 1987 poll, only 13 percent of the American public admits to coming face-to-face with a Formerly Alive Person.

On the other hand, ghost stories are a part of nearly every culture

*In Britain ghosts have long been an accepted part of the landscape. Parapsychologists there have counted some 18,000 spectres. The British Tourist Authority provides information on where they can supposedly be spotted.*

in the world, and have been around as long as language has. Ghosts turn up regularly in literature, too, from *Hamlet* to *Ghostbusters*, from "A Christmas Carol" to *Casper*, from *Blithe Spirit* to *Ghost Dad*.

But ghosts are something more than just the stuff of stories. For twenty-five centuries or more, historians and scientists, law enforcement officers and parapsychologists (those who study unusual and unexplained phenomena) have been investigating and recording real-life ghostly encounters. Often these encounters involve dozens of credible witnesses.

How closely do real-life accounts match the concept of ghosts put forth by Shakespeare and Dickens and Hollywood? Decide for yourself, by testing your Ghost IQ. (Answers are below.)

|  | T | F |
|---|---|---|
| 1) Ghosts appear only at night, preferably around midnight. | ☐ | ☐ |
| 2) The best place to look for a ghost is in a graveyard or a deserted mansion. | ☐ | ☐ |
| 3) The most fashionable ghosts wear long, flowing, white garments. | ☐ | ☐ |
| 4) You know when you're looking at a ghost because you can see right through it, and it doesn't cast a shadow. | ☐ | ☐ |
| 5) Cats and dogs react to the presence of ghosts. | ☐ | ☐ |
| 6) If friends are with you, they'll be able to see the ghost, too. | ☐ | ☐ |
| 7) You can't touch a ghost; your hand passes right through it. | ☐ | ☐ |
| 8) A ghost can't touch you, either. | ☐ | ☐ |
| 9) A ghost can't communicate with you. | ☐ | ☐ |
| 10) A person who met a violent death is a prime candidate for ghosthood. | ☐ | ☐ |

Answers: 1) F 2) F 3) F 4) F 5) T 6) F 7) T 8) F 9) F 10) T

Actually, the above test is a bit unfair. Not all ghosts are created equal. In fact, they come in so many varieties that there are very few hard-and-fast rules about them.

They can be put into several very loose classifications. But before we start classifying ghosts, we need to make a distinction between ghosts and spirits.

Spirits, as defined by parapsychologist Hans Holzer, are the surviving personalities of people who have died "in a reasonably normal fashion" and passed on to the next world. (For one theory about what the next world is like, see the volume in this series titled *Long-Ago Lives*.)

Some people believe we can communicate with the spirits of the dead through psychic individuals called mediums. This belief, called Spiritualism, was especially widespread in the last half of the nineteenth century. Many well-known and well-respected people consulted mediums in an attempt to contact the spirits of loved ones.

Ghosts (also called spooks, spectres, phantoms, and phantasms) are an entirely different species. Because there are so many different kinds, it's hard to state with any authority what a ghost *is*. Hans Holzer defines them as "the surviving emotional memories of people who have died tragically and are unaware of their own passing." Unlike spirits, they haven't made the transition to the next world; they're still tied to this one, usually by some unfinished business.

That does describe one type of ghost—probably the type that most people think of when they hear the term *ghost*. But Holzer's definition doesn't fit all ghosts by any means.

For one thing, not every ghost is an ethereal remnant of a dead person. And even those that are were not necessarily victims of a tragic death. A few ghosts don't seem to be connected with an actual person at all, living or dead.

Obviously we need a broader definition than Holzer's. Modern parapsychologists sometimes refer to ghosts as "discarnate entities"—in other words, something that looks or behaves like a person, but has no physical reality, no body. Not everyone agrees with that, either, as you'll see, but it may be as close as we can get to a definition.

One thing all ghosts have in common: they don't have to be summoned, as spirits do. Ghosts show up uninvited—sometimes, it seems, in order to deliberately annoy the living.

It's almost as tough to pigeonhole ghosts as it is to define them. Some parapsychologists divide ghosts into three broad categories: apparitions, poltergeists, and hauntings. We'll look at some of each.

There are thousands of gripping ghost stories from all over the world and from all time periods, but most are mere tales or legends, or else they depend on the testimony of just one witness, often a very upset and incoherent one.

The accounts you'll read in this book are more than just spooky stories. Nearly all involve multiple witnesses, and most were thoroughly investigated by levelheaded, knowledgeable people. And that makes them all the more compelling.

# PART ONE

# Apparitions

*This photograph, taken at Raynham Hall in Norfolk, England, in 1936, is considered by some to be a genuine picture of an apparition known as the Brown Lady. According to legend, the appearance of the Brown Lady foretells a death in the family.*

# Dead or Alive

Basically, the term *apparition* just refers to a ghost you can see. Apparitions come in several forms: a moving light or ball of light; a white mist, more or less human shaped; a human figure that's two-dimensional, like a projected image; or a very solid-looking and real-seeming figure.

The first two types are too iffy to deserve much discussion. Since they're not recognizably human, it's easy to dismiss them as marsh gas, ball lightning, fog, or hallucinations.

The two-dimensional figure is suspect, too. It may not be a ghost in the usual sense but something called a psychic imprint. This is a sort of residue of energy left behind by someone who died in that spot. A sensitive or psychic person may pick up that energy and get a "picture" of the dead person from it. To help you grasp this concept, think about how living people leave a scent imprint that a human can't smell but a dog's more sensitive nose can.

Not all apparitions can be explained away as natural phenomena, hallucinations, or residual energy. In some cases, the figure seems to have all the attributes of a living, breathing human being. These are no misty, transparent wraiths, but three-dimensional forms that cast shadows and create a reflection in a mirror. Their footsteps and sometimes their voices echo through rooms. They may leave a scent of tobacco or perfume in the air. They may even reach out and touch someone, literally.

And yet, as solid as they seem, they aren't. They fade in and fade out. They walk through walls. Try to touch them and your hand passes through them as if through air. And instead of the warmth of a living body, they bring with them an unnatural chill.

Apparitions appear most often at night, perhaps because the minds of the living are more receptive then, when there are fewer distractions. But there's no shortage of daytime apparitions.

The broad category of apparitions can be broken down into two subcategories: apparitions of the living and apparitions of the dead.

We're used to thinking of ghosts in terms of dead people. But many apparitions have all the qualities of the usual ghost except for one thing: the apparent—the person the ghost resembles—is very much alive. Some call this kind of apparition a double; others prefer the German term *doppelgänger*, which means "double-walker." In Victorian England, it was called a fetch and was said to be an omen that the apparent would soon die.

Early in his presidency, Abraham Lincoln, a great believer in omens, saw a double of himself next to his real reflection in a mirror. He took this to mean that he'd die during his second term—which he did.

Often, though, rather than bringing bad news, a double can be a blessing. When nineteenth-century author Guy de Maupassant

*When the Reverend K. F. Lord snapped this picture of the altar of Newby Church in Yorkshire, England, in 1963, he didn't notice the ghostly figure on the right. It turned up on the finished print.*

was having trouble finishing a story, he was visited by an image of himself, which proceeded to dictate a very satisfactory ending.

In some cases, the apparent isn't even aware of the double. In 1846, girls at a private school in Latvia, a country in central Europe, were practicing embroidery while their French teacher, Emilie Sagée, picked flowers outside. At the same moment, Mlle Sagée also appeared in a chair at the front of the classroom. After several similarly startling incidents, disturbed parents called for the teacher's dismissal. It was the nineteenth time in sixteen years that poor Mlle Sagée had lost a job because of her uncanny ability to be in two places at once—which would seem to be a valuable quality in a teacher.

A double can also turn up far away from the apparent. While on a trip to Egypt in 1864, Mrs. E. H. Elgee was visited by a lifelike likeness of a friend back in England. She knew it was no dream, because her roommate saw it, too. When Mrs. Elgee returned home, her friend revealed that, on the night his double appeared, he had been fretting over some personal crisis and wishing Mrs. Elgee were there to advise him.

# Short-Lived Spectres

Many apparitions are, like the one Mrs. Elgee saw, brought about by some disturbance in the life of the apparent. More often they're created by the apparent's death, particularly when it's a sudden or violent one. Apparitions of the dead fall into three categories:

1) *crisis apparitions*, which appear less than twelve hours after death

2) *postmortem apparitions*, which appear twelve hours or more after death

3) *continual* or *recurrent apparitions*, which come back again and again, sometimes over a period of many years

Crisis apparitions are by far the most common. In 1886, the British Society for Psychical Research published a book containing 701 of the most convincing reports of "phantasms." Well over half were crisis apparitions.

In several cases, the apparition conveyed some information that the person who saw it couldn't have known otherwise. This is called a veridical apparition. One such case involved a Scottish schoolboy,

*The vast majority of postmortem and crisis apparitions involve dead friends and family members. In 1991 this two-year-old began pointing into thin air and insisting that "Old Nanna"—his deceased great-grandmother—was in the room.*

G. F. Russell Colt. In 1855, the figure of Russell's older brother Oliver appeared in the boy's room, gazing "lovingly, imploringly and sadly" at him. That wouldn't have been so unusual, except that Oliver was in Turkey at the time, fighting in the Crimean War. To Russell's horror, blood was gushing from a wound on his brother's right temple. Two weeks later, the family got word that Oliver had died while storming a Turkish fort. He'd been shot in the right temple.

A similar encounter took place in Camden, New Jersey, in 1856. Anne Collyer woke to find her son Joseph standing in her bedroom doorway, staring at her—though she knew he was a thousand miles away, commanding a steamboat on the Mississippi River. Joseph wore a soiled white nightshirt, and his head was wrapped in a bloody bandage. It was two weeks before Mrs. Collyer learned that, on the night the apparition appeared, Joseph's boat had been wrecked. A broken mast had fallen and crushed his skull. At the time of the accident, her son, who had been asleep, had come on deck dressed in his nightshirt.

Most crisis apparitions make no attempt to communicate with the living; they just appear briefly, then disappear. But occasionally, the ghost of the departed speaks to or even touches the living. In 1884, an Englishman named Griffiths was heading home after visiting his fiancée in France. On the way he heard the girl's voice pleading with him in French to return to Paris. Then an exact image of her appeared and clutched his arm. In the morning, he found a red, blistered spot on the arm, as if he'd been burned. Later that day, Griffiths received a telegram from Paris, with the news that his fiancée had died suddenly in the night—after calling out the very words Griffiths had heard.

One of the best-documented conversations with an apparition took place just after World War I, at an English airfield. Pilot J. J. Larkin was sitting in his quarters when his roommate, Lieutenant David McConnel, entered, dressed in his flying clothes. Larkin was surprised to see him because McConnel was supposed to be flying a plane to another airfield. "Back already?" said Larkin.

"Yes," McConnel replied. "Got there all right, had a good trip. Well, cheerio." Shortly after McConnel left, Larkin noted the time: 3:45 P.M. That evening, Larkin learned that McConnel's plane had taken off as scheduled but then crashed, killing the pilot. McConnel's smashed wristwatch had stopped at 3:25 P.M.

All of the above episodes happened at the time of the apparent's death or soon afterward. But many apparitions appear weeks, months, even years after the physical body bites the dust. In 1957, two women in Helsinki shared an elevator with a polite passenger

Most ghosts turn up not in graveyards but in the places they frequented in life. This 1959 photo was taken at a ceremonial site used by Australian aboriginal (native) people. The photographer saw nothing but trees.

who was a dead ringer for the prime minister of Finland, Dr. Juho Passikivi. But Passikivi had died four months earlier. "Ladies," said the late prime minister, who was but a ghost of his former self, "you will certainly wonder why I am here when I should be in a grave." Before he could explain further, the elevator stopped, and the apparition stepped off and disappeared.

Another incident that took place in the 1950s had only one witness, but he was a very credible one—American archaeologist Leon Weeks. Whenever a scientist reports a ghost, it's worth noting. Because they risk being laughed at by their colleagues, most scientists won't speak up unless they're sure of what they saw.

What Weeks saw, at an archaeological dig on Turkey's Gallipoli Peninsula, was a figure in a World War I uniform, leading a donkey with another soldier tied to its back. It wasn't until 1968 that Weeks learned who the figure was: a stretcher bearer in the Australian army named Kirkpatrick. He had rescued hundreds of wounded men during the 1915 attack on Gallipoli before being killed himself and buried there.

# Persistent Phantasms

Though Weeks saw the spectre of Kirkpatrick and his donkey several nights in a row, it was more in the nature of a onetime postmortem apparition than a recurrent one. Recurrent apparitions turn up at one spot repeatedly over a period of months or years, and are seen by many independent witnesses.

Sometimes we describe the spots where apparitions recur as "haunted" places. But, as you'll see in part three, *haunted* has a different, more specific meaning in the language of parapsychology. Unlike haunts, recurrent apparitions usually don't interact with the living or even seem aware of them, and they seem to have no particular purpose. They just repeat the same behavior over and over without variation, like an instant replay.

The prize for most persistent apparition may well go to the ghost of a man on horseback that has been riding about southwestern England for centuries. From his appearance, historians guess that he dates back to the Bronze Age, which makes him at least 2,500 years old. A close runner-up is the Roman legionnaire who once patrolled

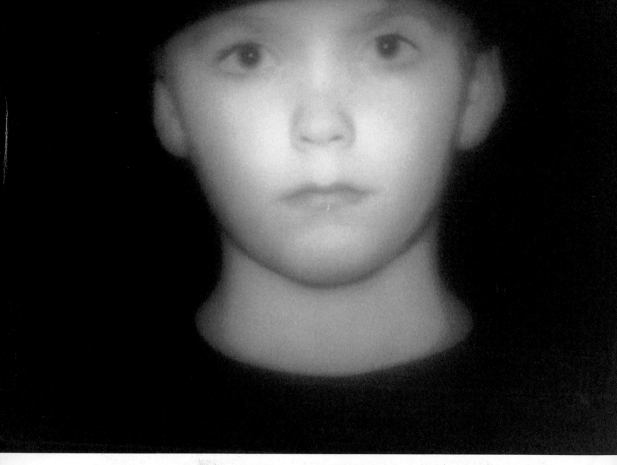

*American parapsychologist William G. Roll believes that an apparition is somehow created by the percipient—the person who observes it—to satisfy some emotional need, such as the desire to see a dead loved one.*

a burial mound in Wales, his golden armor gleaming in the dark. In the early 1800s, archaeologists dug up the mound and found, among the many skeletons, one of a tall man in gold-plated armor of a type used by Roman troops in the first century. Though his ghost no longer walks, the soldier's bones and armor are still on display at the British Museum.

Since America was settled so much later than Britain, its ghosts tend to be of a more recent vintage. The most violent periods of history seem to yield the most ghosts, so it's not surprising that many of America's apparitions date from Civil War days or the time of the Wild West.

Fort Laramie, Wyoming, is home to several ghosts, but the most memorable is the Woman in Green. Every seven years, she's seen galloping a black horse across the plains near the fort. The most reliable sighting was reported in 1871, by Lieutenant James Allison. Allison rode after the young woman, trying to catch her. But when he topped a rise he found that she had vanished, leaving no tracks. The lieutenant's dog was cowering and whining, refusing to trail the ghost. Allison later learned that the Sioux Indians in the area had been seeing the Woman in Green for at least twenty years. According to local legend, she was an officer's daughter who wanted to marry a man her father disapproved of. Furious, she galloped off and was never seen again—except in ghostly form.

A woman dressed in blue has been the resident ghost at Fort Hays, Kansas, for over a century. In 1917, a farmer tried to speak to her, but his horse wouldn't go near her. Forty years later, a policeman ran through her with his patrol car. In 1977, she shook up a farmworker so badly that he nearly fell from a ladder.

Most locals believe she's the ghost of Elizabeth Polly, the wife of an outfitter at the fort. When a cholera epidemic swept through the fort in 1867, Elizabeth lovingly nursed the sick soldiers until she died of the disease herself. Elizabeth had loved to stroll along the bluffs near the fort. After she died she was buried on top of the cliffs. A monument to her still stands there.

Not all recurrent apparitions have as compelling a history as Elizabeth Polly or as prolonged an existence as the Roman sentry. An apparition that spooked employees at a Virginia radio station hung around for only seven months. In 1980, workers at the station began encountering the insubstantial figure of a former employee who had died two years before. The station manager called in parapsychologists from the Psychical Research Foundation in Durham, North Carolina, who interviewed the witnesses. Three of them, it turned out, were having emotional problems (aside from those brought on by seeing a ghost!), and three showed some evidence of psychic sensitivity.

This meshes with the findings of other parapsychologists, who conclude that, as with two-dimensional "psychic imprints," apparitions tend to turn up in the presence of people with some psychic ability.

# Phantom Pets

Terrified animals such as Lieutenant Allison's dog or the Kansas farmer's horse are a common feature of ghost stories, and possibly a significant one. Some parapsychologists believe that if a cat or dog or other animal reacts strongly to a ghost, this is compelling evidence that the apparition is something more than a hallucination.

Animals figure prominently in the history of ghosts in another way, too. Occasionally, the apparition itself is an animal, not a human. One of the most-witnessed animal apparitions was a Newfoundland dog named Mungo. The dog had once belonged to an officer in the Dutch army. Both dog and master died, but Mungo's ghost apparently remained attached to his old company. In the 1800s, when the Netherlands was at war with Belgium, Mungo wandered about the Dutch camp at night, nudging sentries awake before the captain of the guard caught them napping.

In 1916, Albert Payson Terhune, author of such classic dog stories as *Lad of Sunnybank*, was visited by the ghost of a dead pet. As Terhune was talking to a houseguest, the visitor noticed an

*Animal apparitions have been around as long as human ones. This "ghost dog" appeared in a 1916 photograph without the photographer's knowledge. Considering how long film had to be exposed at that time, it's possible that a real dog momentarily entered the frame.*

unfamiliar dog peering through the window. The dog vanished before Terhune got a look at it, but the visitor's description matched Terhune's dog Rex exactly, down to the large scar on his face. Rex had died earlier that year.

# Homemade Spooks

There's even evidence that some people, by concentrating long and hard enough, can actually *create* a recurrent apparition. Eastern mystics call this sort of manufactured ghost a *tulpa*. Early in this century, French journalist Alexandra David-Neel saw Tibetan monks accomplish this and tried it herself. After meditating for several months, David-Neel conjured up the *tulpa* of a fat, jolly monk. At first, the monk was pleasant company, but as time went on, he developed a darker side and a "vaguely mocking, sly, malignant look." Alarmed, David-Neel decided, like Dr. Frankenstein, to destroy her creation. She succeeded, but only after six months of intense mental effort.

If an apparition can be created, does that mean that all apparitions are nothing more than a figment of the viewer's imagination? There are those who think so. They point to the fact that our minds have a way of playing tricks on us. If we're in the right surroundings or the right frame of mind, they say, we can see things that aren't there or look at some ordinary object and see a ghost.

In 1960, A. D. Cornell, a member of the British Society for Psychical Research, devised an experiment to determine just how suggestible the average person really is. One evening, he draped himself in a white sheet and wandered about the churchyard of Saint Peter's Church in Cambridge, moaning appropriately. Of the ninety motorists, forty bicyclists, and twelve pedestrians who passed, only two took any notice. When asked what he thought he'd seen, one said, "An art student walking around in a blanket." The other said, "A man dressed up as a woman who surely must be mad." So much for suggestibility.

Few parapsychologists buy the notion that apparitions are totally imaginary. But many have suggested that apparitions aren't "real" in a physical sense. They've used a variety of terms to try to describe the nature of apparitions: thought-forms, psychic holograms, telepathic perceptions, ESP hallucinations. All these terms imply that an apparition has no existence independent of the person who's seeing or sensing it.

Another group of experts takes the opposite view: apparitions, they say, are independent entities. They consist of the soul or personality of a dead person, housed in an "ultraphysical" form. This form may be called a soul body, an etheric body, or an apparitional body.

Others think the truth may lie in some combination of the two theories. Perhaps apparitions are independent entities, but they can't be seen physically, only psychically—that is, not with the eyes but with some "sixth sense."

Of course, there's no reason to assume that all apparitions are the same. Some may well be more "real" and independent than others.

Certainly that seems to be true of ghosts in general. Some are

*When this photograph of England's Eastry Church was taken in 1956, no one was in the pews—at least no one living.*

far more substantial than others. Apparitions are a relatively weak species of spectre. The ghosts that make the strongest impression on the living are poltergeists and haunts.

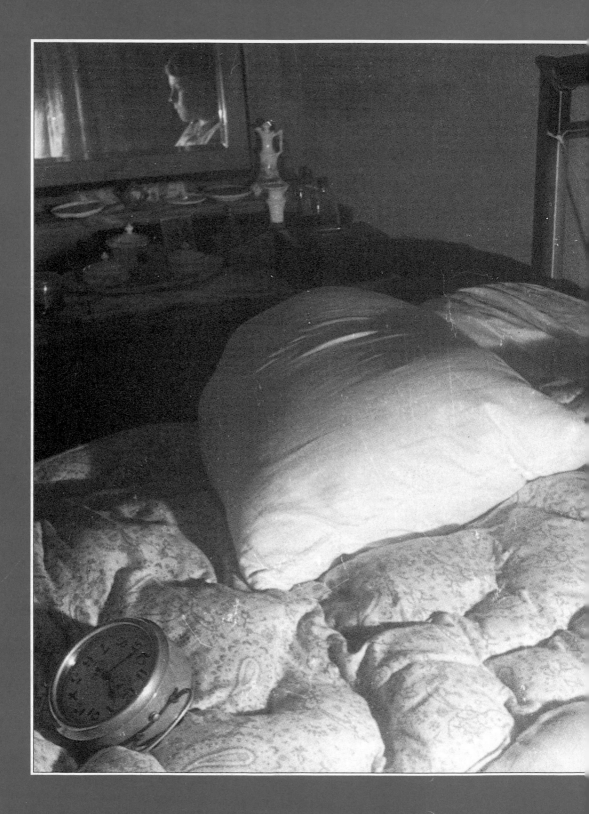

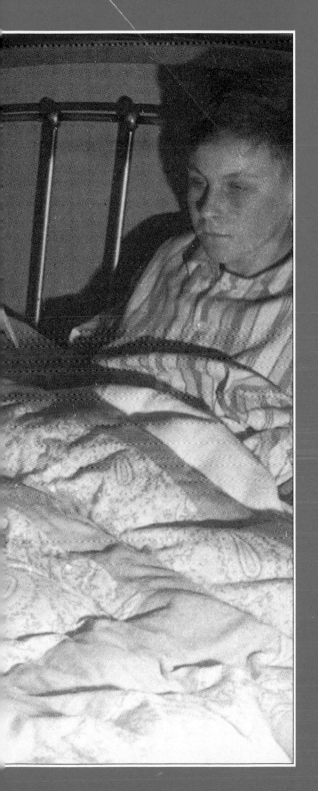

# PART TWO

# Poltergeists

# I Was a Teenage Poltergeist

Poltergeists are at the opposite end of the ghostly spectrum from apparitions. Apparitions are mostly seen but not heard or felt. A poltergeist's presence is felt and heard but seldom seen. Though the German term *poltergeist* means "noisy ghost," many experts don't consider them ghosts at all, at least not according to the definition offered earlier — a discarnate entity. These parapsychologists point out that poltergeist activity usually centers around a living person they call the poltergeist agent. Most often the agent is a teenage girl, but sometimes it's a boy.

One theory is that, because of their raging hormones, teens are filled with so much emotional energy—and so much hostility—that it can actually leak out into their surroundings, causing loud noises and tossing objects around. Some say the force that does the tossing is a form of psychokinesis—the ability, in this case on the part of the teenager, to move objects without touching them. (See *Paranormal Powers* in this series.)

Certainly the "disturbed teen" theory fits a lot of poltergeist

*Joseph Priestley called the poltergeist incident at Epworth Rectory "the best authenticated and the best told story of the kind."*

cases. Joseph Priestley, the English scientist who discovered oxygen, was probably the first to suggest that poltergeist activity might be caused by the living. Priestley had studied a celebrated incident that took place before he was born. It occurred at Epworth Rectory, the boyhood home of John Wesley, the founder of Methodism. John's father, the Reverend Samuel Wesley, was also a clergyman. Though John was a teenager at the time of the disturbances, no one suspected him of being responsible for them; he was away at boarding school.

The activity centered around one of John's sisters, nineteen-year-old Hetty. Some modern scholars have accused Hetty of causing the commotion deliberately, through some kind of trickery or sleight of hand. Though Hetty was a clever girl, it's doubtful that she was clever enough to pull off some of the poltergeist's stunts.

The incident started in December 1716 in the same way most poltergeist cases begin—with knocking sounds on the floors and walls of the house. Then came footsteps and loud rumblings, sounds like the crashing of glass and the clinking of coins. The family searched the house, but found nothing that would account for the racket. Each time someone suggested that the sounds were due to natural causes, they increased, as if in protest.

When Samuel Wesley angrily challenged the "deaf and dumb devil," it began to play rough. An invisible hand shoved him into doors and desks. At meals, his plate of food danced across the table. Friends advised Wesley to abandon the rectory, but the reverend stubbornly refused.

Once the Wesley daughters grew used to the invisible presence, they seemed to relish the excitement it caused, and fondly dubbed it Old Jeffery. Hetty was the only one who claimed to have actually seen Old Jeffery; she described him as an old man in a long white robe that dragged on the floor.

Hetty was always present when the noises began, and sometimes they seemed to follow her around the house. But it wasn't until Priestley studied the case decades later that anyone accused her of being somehow responsible for the poltergeist.

The Epworth disturbances stopped abruptly after two months. A century later, the Bell family of Tennessee entertained an even more obnoxious unseen visitor for a long and exhausting three years!

Though the ghost in this case is commonly called the Bell Witch, it's a classic example of a poltergeist, with a few added attractions. The incident began as the Epworth case did, with strange rappings and scratchings. But the poltergeist quickly stepped up its attack, yanking the bedclothes off sleeping family members, pulling their hair, slapping their faces. At first, Betsy Bell, a pretty, cheerful twelve-year-old, seemed to be the main target of the mischief. When she was sent to stay briefly with a neighbor, the noises followed her— but at the same time, they kept up at the Bells' house.

At the family's request, James Johnson, a lay preacher, brought in a committee of local residents to investigate. They concluded that, whatever the poltergeist was, it was no hoax. There seemed to be a conscious entity at work, which they dubbed a witch. As word of the strange shenanigans spread, crowds of the curious came from all over, encouraging the "witch" to put on a more dramatic show. When spoken to, it responded with raps that indicated "yes" or "no," then with a low whistling sound that evolved into whispered words. Once it found its voice, the poltergeist became unbearable, shrieking and laughing maniacally at all hours.

Among the Bells' visitors was future president Andrew Jackson. When his wagon mysteriously halted on the way and couldn't be budged, Jackson cried, "By the Eternal, it's the witch!" Jackson had brought along a man called a witch-layer, the nineteenth-century version of a ghostbuster. When they reached the Bells' house, the witch-layer tried to shoot the intruder. But an invisible hand seized the man's nose and slapped him about until he fled in terror.

*In the nineteenth century, poltergeist activity was often attributed to an evil spirit, or even to the devil. A priest might be called in to perform an exorcism, a religious rite designed to dispel demons.*

The ghost continued to plague Betsy, who was now fifteen, pleading with her not to marry a neighbor who had been courting her. But it took to tormenting her father, too, so persistently that he broke down and finally died. At the funeral, the "witch" sang coarse songs. After that, it seemed to lose interest in the Bells. The disturbances tapered off and finally stopped altogether.

Was Betsy somehow behind all the uproar? It's impossible to know for sure. Certainly it's hard to imagine how she could have faked it all without anyone noticing. Psychologist Nandor Fodor suggests that Betsy's adolescent energy was the source of the poltergeist's power. But Fodor feels that, like David-Neel's *tulpa*, the ghost somehow took on a life of its own.

# Electrifying Evidence

In several more recent cases, it seems much clearer that a specific agent was the source of the poltergeist activity. In 1967, the warehouse of a souvenir company in Miami was plagued by a poltergeist that sent cartons of back scratchers, mugs, and ashtrays tumbling from the shelves, and soda bottles flying from the hands of startled employees. The police were baffled, so the company turned to the Psychical Research Foundation. Their investigators fingered an employee, a nineteen-year-old Cuban refugee named Julio. Psychological tests revealed that the boy was having severe emotional problems.

This seems to reinforce the "disturbed teen" theory. But let's not jump to conclusions. As parapsychologist Richard S. Broughton says, "If poltergeist outbreaks are simply due to young people with repressed hostility who are under psychological stress, we should expect to see whole school buildings come crashing down by the dozens each year around exam time."

A number of cases suggest that it may not be psychological energy at work, but some form of electrical energy, possibly generated

*Many scientists subscribe to the "principle of least astonishment." Any natural explanation for a phenomenon, they say, is better than a supernatural one. Such scientists feel that unusually high charges of static electricity may be responsible for making objects fly about.*

by the poltergeist agent. This may sound far-fetched, but the fact is, there are a few extraordinary people who seem to carry around an unbelievably high charge of static electricity in their bodies—as much as 30,000 volts. (See *Paranormal Powers* in this series.)

Electrical energy has long been a suspect in poltergeist cases. In 1867, H. A. Willis of Boston found that the knockings and ringing bells and flying crockery in his home seemed linked to a servant girl named Mary. Suspecting that some form of electricity was at work, he placed Mary's bedposts and chair legs atop glass insulators, so they wouldn't be grounded. When Mary sat on those pieces of furniture, the disturbances all but stopped.

*At least forty people witnessed the strange goings-on at the law office in Rosenheim, Germany, in 1967. Investigators captured on film the unexplained gyrations of the ceiling lights.*

A 1967 case at a law office in Rosenheim, Germany, revolved around an eighteen-year-old secretary named Annemarie. Her presence set off all sorts of strange activity, much of it involving electrical appliances. Ceiling lamps swung wildly. File drawers leaped out, and pictures spun on the walls. Phones went dead or dialed numbers without human assistance. Electrical fuses flew from their sockets. Developing fluid spilled from copy machines.

*Sigmund Adam, the lawyer who employed Annemarie, displays a printed record of the strange behavior exhibited by his office phone.*

Electrical engineers were stymied; so were the police. It took two physicists and a poltergeist investigator to zero in on Annemarie as the cause of it all. When she left to take another job, the disturbances stopped. She shook up her new office a little at first, but gradually those problems died out, too.

A similar set of troubles began for a Polish girl named Joasia in 1983, when she was thirteen. First, her friends noticed that she seemed to actually crackle with static electricity. Then objects began flying around her family's apartment—plates, glasses, knives, even furniture. When a team of scientists tested Joasia, they found unusually warm areas on her body, large and rapid changes in her overall body temperature, and an amazingly high charge of static electricity.

In these three modern cases, teens were again the agents. But there have been plenty of poltergeist incidents in which no teens were on the scene. In a 1967 English case (1967 seems to have been a good year for poltergeists!), the spectral thumpings were so violent that they knocked a hole in a plaster wall. Predictably, the noises seemed to center around a young boy. But what baffled parapsychologists was the fact that the uproar continued after the boy and his family moved out.

In 1981, a widow in Bakersfield, California, tried to redecorate the house she'd bought. Something invisible responded by banging windows and doors and knocking pictures from the walls. The widow suspected it was the ghost of the former owner, protesting the changes.

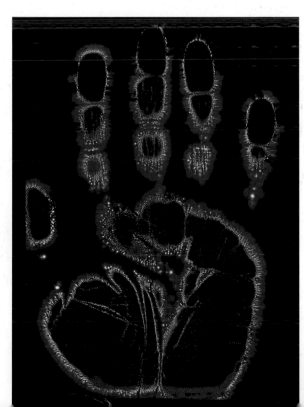

*Subjects captured by a technique called Kirlian photography, or electrophotography, seem to be surrounded by a glow, or aura. Some parapsychologists claim this is a measure of the subject's psychic energy.*

# Knocks and Rocks

In some cases, poltergeist activity doesn't revolve around a particular agent at all. A surprising number of these cases involve a phenomenon known as lithobolia—stones falling from the sky or from the ceiling of a house. Oddly enough, the victims of these stone showers are seldom seriously injured. Often the rocks seem to float rather than plummet to the ground or the floor. The stones that pelted the Lowe family in 1962 traveled at an angle, like wind-driven snowflakes. Some were warm to the touch.

In other poltergeist cases, witnesses have noticed that the flying objects, whether rocks or crockery, often change speed and direction in midair. Antics like these, which seem to defy the laws of physics, have convinced some parapsychologists that the objects aren't just flying around at random but are being controlled by some invisible entity, separate from the poltergeist agent.

Usually the knocks that are heard are more than just random noises, too. As in the Bell Witch case, they often seem to respond to the actions or words of the living. A number of investigators have

*Reports of stone-throwing poltergeists date back to at least A.D. 530. The 1849 outbreak in France depicted here was linked to a servant girl who was present during the attacks.*

had the presence of mind to communicate with the ghost through a rapping code, of the sort used by mediums to get messages from spirits—usually one knock for "yes" and two for "no."

One of the earliest cases of this kind happened in 1761, to a London family named Parsons. As usual, the disturbance centered around a teenager, thirteen-year-old Elizabeth. Her father tore the wainscoting off the walls in an attempt to find the source of the noises. When that failed, he called in the Reverend John Moore, a minister who had read of the strange events at John Wesley's home forty-five years earlier.

Moore communicated with the ghost by using a code of raps. The ghost identified itself as Fanny Kent, who had once rented a room in the house. According to "Scratching Fanny," as she was now known, she'd been poisoned by her brother-in-law, William Kent.

Indignant, William Kent sued the Parsons family, accusing them of faking the whole thing because they had a grudge against him. Though Parsons and his wife were found guilty, many of those who witnessed the rap sessions were convinced that "Scratching Fanny" was no hoax.

A 1980 French poltergeist communicated not through a code or through spoken language, but through symbols—triangles, circles, and crosses scrawled on the floor and on the thigh of the poltergeist agent, a woman named Carla. Carla's husband tried to photograph the poltergeist in action, but when he opened the camera to remove the roll of film, he found instead a folded piece of paper with the same familiar designs on it.

Some parapsychologists believe that poltergeists, like other

Parapsychologist Hans Bender attempts to communicate psychically with the French poltergeist, using a board on which messages are spelled out.

In addition to the standard poltergeist activity such as moving tables, lifting rugs, and punching and pinching people, the "noisy ghost" that plagued a French household in 1980 was fond of scrawling strange symbols.

ghosts, are discarnate entities. These researchers agree that an emotionally disturbed person, especially a teen, may be the root of the problem. But they suggest that the energy given off by the disturbed person, rather than actually causing the phenomena, may be providing a kind of psychic fuel supply. A ghost that's too weak to make its presence known is drawn to that free-floating emotional energy like a moth to a porch light, and draws enough power from it to make a nuisance of itself.

Many so-called poltergeists, of course, prove to be out-and-out frauds. The disturbances often turn out to be perpetrated by a teenager seeking attention. In 1984, the Resch family of Columbus, Ohio, was tormented by moving furniture, smashed picture frames, and flying phone receivers. When investigators placed hidden cameras about the house, they caught the culprit red-handed—the Resches' fourteen-year-old adopted daughter, Tina. She was frustrated because her family opposed her efforts to locate her birth parents.

Skeptics say that if poltergeist activity isn't faked, it must necessarily be due to natural phenomena—the wind rattling a shutter, the house settling, animals scampering around in the attic, and the like. British researcher G. W. Lambert found that many houses where paranormal goings-on were reported were located near or on underground streams. When the water level rose, he said, it caused the house to shift, moving objects and causing noises. Others were near geological faults. In these houses, most of the reports came during periods of earthquake activity.

Certainly a slight earth tremor might send unstable objects tumbling from shelves. And an old house shifting and settling does

*Most so-called poltergeist activity proves to be faked or caused by natural phenomena. But every few years parapsychologists encounter a case that can't be easily explained, such as the 1985 incident that trashed this home in England.*

give off some strange sounds. And animals scrabbling around could be mistaken for something unearthly.

But tremors don't send stones raining from the ceiling, and creaking floor joists don't respond to questions, and, unless they're cartoon characters, mice and squirrels don't pull down bedclothes or push people around or slap their faces.

So who's right? Are poltergeists really mischievous ghosts, or natural phenomena, or frustrated teens? Maybe, as with apparitions, there is no single explanation. There's obviously more than one brand of poltergeist, so why shouldn't there be more than one explanation? Noted researcher Ian Stevenson puts it more succinctly: "Some poltergeists are living and others are dead."

# PART THREE

# Hauntings

# Rubber Bands
# and Revenge

There are lots of conflicting theories about the nature of hauntings, too. There are even different ideas about what a haunting is. Places where apparitions turn up regularly are commonly called haunted. So are houses with a record of poltergeist activity.

But most parapsychologists consider a haunting a separate phenomenon. It's probably best described as a cross between an apparition and a poltergeist. Like apparitions, haunts can be seen, they can hang around for years or even centuries, they turn up more often at night than in the daytime, they're often accompanied by strange smells and an uncanny feeling of cold, and animals tend to be terror-stricken by them. Like poltergeists, haunts make noises, though usually more subdued ones, they move objects around, and they may communicate with the living.

Skeptical scholars look to natural phenomena as a way of explaining hauntings, too, and sometimes they turn out to be right. But in many hauntings, if not most, there's a clear connection between the haunt and some person who met an unhappy or violent end on the premises.

One of the oldest hauntings on record was described by Roman scholar Pliny the Younger in the first century. It has all the elements of the classic haunting. In fact, the ghost bears a close family resemblance to the ghost of Marley in "A Christmas Carol."

A "large and handsome house" in Athens, Greece, was for rent cheap, but, because it was said to be haunted, no one would have it except the philosopher Athenodorus. Late one night, the figure of an old man appeared in the house. His white hair and beard were long and matted, and his wrists and ankles were shackled with clanking chains. The ghost beckoned, and Athenodorus followed it outside, where it pointed to a spot in the garden, then vanished. The next morning, the philosopher had the spot dug up and found a skeleton bound by rusted chains. When the bones were given a proper burial, the hauntings ceased.

Athenodorus's haunt had a definite purpose in mind, and that's true of many hauntings. Occasionally, the purpose is something absurdly simple. Lady Harris, an Englishwoman, was haunted by the ghost of her house's former owner, who seemed to be searching for something. When Lady Harris learned that the man had had a habit of tying up his beard each night with a rubber band, she left one on the dresser. In the morning it was gone. So was the ghost.

*Many haunts seem determined to take care of unfinished business. Often, as in the story of Athenodorus, the ghost wants its physical remains to be given a decent burial.*

Usually a haunt's purpose is more significant. In January 1800, a disembodied voice began speaking to Abner Blaisdel of Machiasport, Maine. The voice claimed to be that of Nelly Butler, a neighbor who had died with her infant in childbirth. By May, the disembodied voice had taken on a body—a ghostly, glowing form in a white gown. Not everyone could see the apparition, but those who could agreed that it was the image of Nelly Butler.

Nelly's main purpose in returning to this world seemed to be to urge her husband, George, to remarry. She even had a match picked out—Abner Blaisdel's daughter Lydia. At first, Lydia refused. "I will not marry a man who has been scared into proposing by a ghost," she said. But when George assured her that he was agreeable, the two married. Neighbors accused Lydia of manufacturing the ghost in order to get a husband. Indignant, Nelly Butler called a large crowd together, then sent Lydia from the room, to show that she could appear with no help from Lydia.

For some reason, Nelly also insisted that the body of her baby be dug up and reburied about thirty feet away. Over the course of a year, the ghost appeared at least twenty-five times, sometimes talking for hours on end to as many as fifty witnesses. Then, apparently feeling she'd accomplished what she came for, she stopped showing up.

The ghost that haunted Ash Manor in Sussex, England, in the 1930s had a more sinister purpose. After several encounters with the ghost—a nasty-looking fellow in a green smock and muddy trousers—the owners of the house appealed to Nandor Fodor at London's International Institute for Psychical Research. Fodor brought along the famous psychic Eileen Garrett, who went into a

*When medium Eileen Garrett (second from left) was brought to Ash Manor, she seemed to take on the identity of the "green man" who haunted the house. The owners claimed that Garrett's features actually transformed so that she resembled the ghost.*

trance and began speaking in a strange voice, using outdated English. The voice claimed to be that of a man named Henley. Both his lands and his wife had been stolen from him, he said, by men he considered his friends. Henley wanted revenge.

Fodor convinced Henley that, as long as he clung to his desire for vengeance, he would stay tied to this world and would never see his wife or his son, who had passed on to the next world. Henley seemed to buy this, and disappeared. But the next night he was back. Eileen Garrett sensed that the owners of the house were disturbed and unhappy, and she felt the ghost was being drawn there by their emotional energy. When the couple broke down and confessed that they were having severe personal problems, the ghost left Ash Manor for good.

# Setting Free the Spooks

Not all haunts have an obvious purpose. Some are just attached to a particular place because they were comfortable and happy there when they were alive. If a living person moves in, the ghost can get very possessive and may even try to chase away the intruder.

Other haunts don't seem to realize they're dead, and go on trying to behave as they did in life. Usually their death was a sudden one. Parapsychologist Ian Currie estimates that over 80 percent of all ghosts are the result of an abrupt demise. "Sudden death," says Currie, "often confuses people." According to English ghosthunter Eddie Burks, ghosts inhabit an "etheric body." This state of being is a sort of stepping-stone between the physical body they had in life and the spiritual body they'll have in the next world.

In the etheric body, a ghost's consciousness is dimmed. The ghost may not realize for a long time what its true situation is. It may go on wandering about aimlessly for years. When it finally dawns on the ghost that it's dead, it may become frustrated, uncertain how to

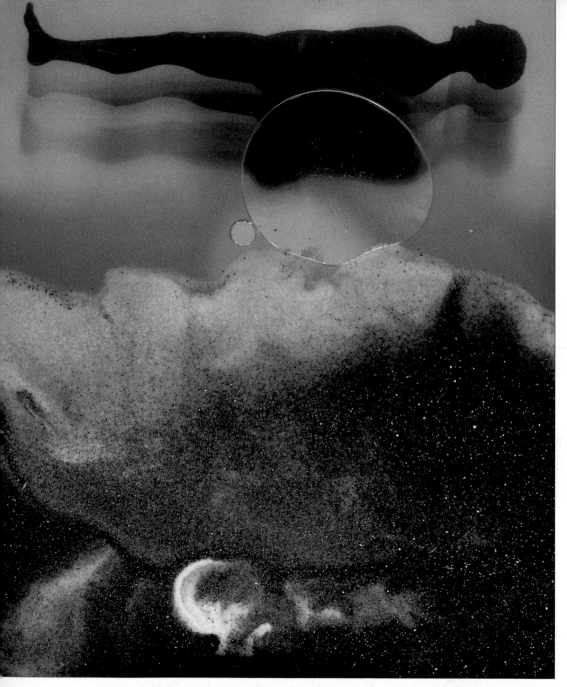

*Ghosthunter Eddie Burks claims that, in one out of every five hundred deaths, the spirit of the deceased refuses to move on to the spirit world because of some strong attachment to the world of the living.*

move on to the next plane of existence. Burks makes it his business to help these "trapped souls."

One ghost that Burks freed had been in that twilight zone between life and afterlife for over four hundred years. In 1992, employees at Couts & Co., the prestigious London bank that handles Queen Elizabeth's accounts, began complaining of a headless figure hanging about the entrance and reception area. The temperature of the room dropped sharply when the figure was around; sometimes lights and computers went on the blink.

Burks is one of those sensitive individuals who can sense the presence of ghosts. In fact, he claims to be able to tune in their thoughts.

When the bank called him in, Burks made contact at once with a man whose speech and dress dated from the days of the *first* Queen Elizabeth. From Burks's description, it seemed clear that the ghost was that of Thomas Howard, duke of Norfolk, who was unjustly executed by the queen in 1571.

Apparently all the duke needed was someone sympathetic to talk to. After he and Burks mentally conversed for a while, Howard let go of the bitterness he'd held on to all those years and was ready to move on into the next world. Since then, no one has reported seeing his ghost.

Burks is just one of a long line of ghostbusters that stretches back for centuries. Unsophisticated societies have traditionally relied on pretty crude methods of chasing off unwanted ghosts: brandishing axes, wearing scary masks, setting off firecrackers. Our own practice of wearing black after a funeral probably stems from the ancient belief

*One of the world's best-known ghostbusters was Harry Price, who investigated England's heavily haunted Borley Rectory in the 1930s. Price's ghosthunting kit included cameras, a measuring tape, a simple motion detector, a flask of brandy, and felt overshoes for moving about silently.*

that wearing black makes the living invisible to the dead.

In Christian countries, ghosts were once associated with evil spirits, and people looked to the church to get rid of them. For many years during the Middle Ages, Romans passing by Nero's tomb were tormented by the ghost of the emperor, who committed suicide in A.D. 68. By 1099, the citizens were so upset they appealed to Pope Paschal II for help. The pope cut down the walnut tree that grew on the site, dug up Nero's bones, burned both tree and bones, and threw the ashes in the Tiber River. A drastic method, but it got the ghost's goat, and it never reappeared.

In 1323, Pope John XXII asked the prior of an abbey in Alais, France, to investigate a haunting. The prior brought along a hundred witnesses and three fellow monks, and set about searching the haunted house and the neighboring houses, looking for signs of fraud or possible natural explanations. When the spectre turned up, it proved to be the former owner of the house, who felt he'd been denied entrance into the afterlife because of sins he'd committed in this life. His confession seemed to do the trick; the ghost was never seen again.

The methods used by the prior of Alais nearly seven hundred years ago are remarkably similar to those used by most modern ghostbusters. Some of today's parapsychologists, however, come to a haunting armed with high-tech gear: sensitive recording equipment, denometers that measure electromagnetic activity, thermistors that measure changes in temperature, motion sensors, odor detectors, cameras. In fact, investigators have been using cameras to try to photograph ghosts for a hundred years—and some seem to have actually succeeded.

But when it comes to dealing with ghosts, not just detecting them, high tech isn't necessarily best. Ghostbuster Andrew Green, who was hired to dehaunt London's Albert Hall, has a few weapons, such as a "static electricity dispersal pistol," that bring to mind Hollywood's version of ghostbusting. But most real-life dehaunters take a less combative approach. Instead of gadgetry, they stress the human element. Most rely on mediums to contact ghosts for them.

Once they've got a ghost's attention, the ghostbusters try to convince it that it's dead. That can be tough to do. ("They usually give me an argument," says Ian Currie.) After they've got the spectre straightened out, they ask it to call on a loved one who has died. The loved one acts as a sort of guide, showing the lost soul the way into the next world.

*In 1996, self-described "secular exorcist" Andrew Green, author of* Ghost-Hunting: A Practical Guide, *spent the night at Albert Hall. He saw no sign of the two girls in Victorian garb who reportedly haunt the famous London concert hall.*

# Ghost-Ridden Places

 If you're not a professional ghostbuster, your chances of ever meeting a ghost are pretty slim. Reports of ghosts are definitely on the decline. There are two possible reasons. One is that, because our modern world tends to scoff at the idea of ghosts, those who see them are reluctant to tell anyone about it.

It's also possible that there actually *are* fewer ghosts than there once were, not just fewer reports. After all, the eras that produce the most ghosts are those that produce the most violent, unhappy deaths. Nowadays, most people die in a hospital with their wills made out and their families around them, and are given a proper burial.

Of course, there are still plenty of houses around where someone has met a sudden and tragic end. But noted parapsychologist Hans Holzer estimates that only about 1 percent of them are actually haunted. So, if you're eager to meet a ghost—and not everyone is— where do you start looking? Well, there are a number of places that instead of trying to banish their resident ghosts actually treasure them, usually because they're a tourist attraction.

*According to ghostbusters, ancient, decaying houses hold no special attraction for spooky spectres. Instead, they say, ghosts tend to linger in the places they frequented in life, even though a new building may occupy the spot.*

Great Britain has more than its share of these places: the Tower of London, where the ghosts of Anne Boleyn and Thomas à Becket, Sir Walter Raleigh and Lady Jane Grey are said to walk; Drury Lane Theatre, which boasts some five hundred spectres, including the Man in Gray, whose appearance supposedly signifies that the current production will be a hit; Glamis Castle, the home of half a dozen ghosts including the sixth Lord Glamis's wife, who was burned as a witch in 1537.

*The ghost of Jane Seymour, third wife of King Henry VIII, is said to haunt Hampton Court, the royal residence where she lived.*

Probably the most ghost-ridden building in America is also one of its most famous—the White House. Abigail Adams is sometimes seen in the East Room, where she hung the First Family's wash while the White House was still under construction. Dolley Madison has turned up several times, once when the second Mrs. Woodrow Wilson tried to move the Rose Garden. Dolley protested, and the garden stayed where she had put it. Abraham Lincoln's ghost has been sighted by some very credible witnesses, including Mrs. Calvin Coolidge, Eleanor Roosevelt, and Queen Wilhelmina of the Netherlands, who fainted at the sight.

The Capitol building isn't quite as spook filled, but visitors have reported seeing the ghosts of presidents John Quincy Adams and James Garfield. Apparitions have been spotted in scores of other historic buildings across the country, as well as at the sites of battles, such as Pennsylvania's Gettysburg National Military Park, where ghostly campfires sometimes burn, and Harpers Ferry National Historical Park in West Virginia, which features a regular "ghost tour."

Of course, even if you go where the ghosts are, there's no guarantee you'll encounter one. Not everyone can see or sense a ghost. And that may be just as well. Though there's no record of anyone ever being harmed by an apparition, and there have been few cases of physical injury caused by poltergeists, a run-in with a ghost can be a pretty scary experience. Whatever the true nature of ghosts may be—a hallucination, a concentration of emotional or electrical energy, a psychic imprint, a telepathic image, or the lingering personality of a dead person—there's something about them that sets off an alarm in the nervous system of living people and leaves them shaken up.

So, although ghosts are not something to be feared, neither are they something to be taken lightly. In any case, it's one thing to visit a ghost-ridden place in the company of your family or other tourists and quite another to go exploring a creepy old house on your own. Though you may not stir up any irate spooks, you are likely to upset the living, in the form of the property's owner.

Leave ghostbusting to experienced parapsychologists, and be content to limit your own experience with ghosts to spooky tales told around a campfire.

# Glossary

**apparent:** The person that a double or apparition resembles.

**apparition:** A visible form, usually humanlike, that appears real but takes up no physical space.

**cholera:** An infectious and often deadly disease, usually brought about by eating contaminated food or drinking impure water.

**Crimean War** (1853–1856): A war fought by Russia against Turkey, England, and France to decide who would control the territory around the Black Sea.

**Dickens, Charles** (1812–1870): One of the greatest English novelists, author of such classics as *Oliver Twist, A Tale of Two Cities*, and "A Christmas Carol," plus numerous scary ghost stories.

**double** or *doppelgänger:* A three-dimensional image of a real, living person. Also used in literature to refer to a sort of "evil twin," as in Robert Louis Stevenson's *The Strange Case of Dr. Jekyll and Mr. Hyde.*

**ethereal:** Lacking material substance.

**Gallipoli:** A peninsula in western Turkey, site of a series of bloody battles (1915–1916) during World War I.

**hallucination:** A realistic image created by the mind, not the senses.

**medium:** A person who claims to have the ability to contact the spirits of the dead and speak for them.

**mystic:** A person who claims to understand things that are mysteries to ordinary humans.

**parapsychologist:** A scholar or scientist who studies events outside the usual bounds of science. Fields of parapsychology include extrasensory perception, psychokinesis, and ghosts.

**Pliny the Younger** (about A.D. 61–113): A roman senator and governor whose letters are one of the main sources of information about ancient Rome.

**poltergeist:** A force of unknown origin that creates noises and moves objects.

**Priestley, Joseph** (1733–1804): English scientist, teacher, and religious scholar who experimented with electricity and chemistry, and discovered several gases, including oxygen.

**psychic:** A word used to describe a person who can see or feel things that can't be detected by the usual five senses.

**psychokinesis:** The ability to move or affect objects without touching them.

**rectory:** The home of a clergyman in charge of a parish.

**spirit:** The part of a person that is believed to survive after the physical body dies.

**static electricity:** An electrical charge that builds up in certain materials or in the air. Lightning is a violent form of it.

**telepathic:** A term used to describe thoughts or images that apparently pass from one mind to another without the aid of the usual five senses.

**tulpa:** An independent entity claimed to be created by concentrated and disciplined thought.

**Wesley, John** (1703–1791): English minister who founded the Methodist Church.

# To Learn More about
# Ghosts of All Kinds

## BOOKS-NONFICTION

Clyne, Patricia Edwards. *Strange and Supernatural Animals*. New York: Dodd-Mead, 1979. Varied, well-researched tales of some out-of-the-ordinary animals.

Deem, James M. *How to Find a Ghost*. Boston: Houghton Mifflin, 1988. Very readable advice on where and how to look for ghosts—but downplays the fact that ghosts can be *scary*. Humorous illustrations.

Edwards, Ron. *World's Most Mysterious "True" Ghost Stories*. New York: Sterling, 1996. Thirty-one short tales of disappearances, hauntings, and other mysterious happenings.

Hauck, Dennis William. *National Directory of Haunted Places*. New York: Penguin, 1996. Background information and travel directions for over two thousand places in America where apparitions regularly turn up. Warning: Some of the stories behind the ghosts are gory and unpleasant.

Knight, David C. *The Haunted Souvenir Warehouse*. Garden City, NY: Doubleday, 1978. Eleven detailed accounts of "haunted" places around the world. Maps, photos.

Meier, Gisela. *Ghosts and Poltergeists*. Mankato, MN: Capstone, 1991. A concise overview of apparitions, haunts, and poltergeists.

# BOOKS-FICTION

Coville, Bruce. *The Ghost in the Big Brass Bed.* New York: Bantam, 1991.

———. *The Ghost in the Third Row.* New York: Bantam, 1989.

———. *The Ghost Wore Gray.* New York: Bantam, 1988.
The entertaining adventures of sixth grader Nina Tanleven, amateur ghostbuster.

Seabrook, Brenda. *The Haunting of Holroyd Hill.* New York: Cobblehill, 1995. Melinda and her brother investigate three Civil War–era ghosts that haunt their new home.

Ure, Jean. *The Children Next Door.* New York: Scholastic, 1994. When eleven-year-old Laura spies nonexistent children playing next door, she thinks she's imagining things.


# ORGANIZATIONS

Ghost Research Society, P.O. Box 205, Oak Lawn, IL 60454-0205. Investigates ghosts, hauntings, and poltergeists. Library, speakers' bureau (furnishes names of experts who lecture on ghostly topics), publishes semiannual newsletter, various directories. Annual exhibition/conference.

Haunt Hunters, 509 Big Horn Basin Ct., St. Louis, MO 63011. Collects and provides information about ghosts and other paranormal phenomena. Speakers' bureau, file of case histories.

International Society for the Study of Ghosts and Apparitions, P.O. Box 528124, Chicago, IL 60652-8124. Professional ghosthunters. Library, speakers' bureau. Sponsors Supernatural Mysteries Exposition periodically.

## ON-LINE INFORMATION*

http://www.ghosthunter.org
   Website of the Society for Paranormal Investigation, Research, and Information Training (SPIRIT). News about SPIRIT and information about local society chapters.

http://www.ghostweb.com/
   Official website of the International Ghost Hunters' Society. Extensive gallery of color photos of alleged ghosts; information on IGHS conferences.

*Websites change from time to time. For additional on-line information, check with the media specialist at your local library.

# Index

Page numbers for illustrations are in boldface.

# INDEX

# Notes

Quotes used in this book are from the following sources:

Page 5 "Oh, no": *Ghosts* by the Editors of Time-Life Books (Alexandria, VA: Time-Life, 1984), p. 131.

Page 8 "in a reasonably": *Hans Holzer's Haunted America* by Hans Holzer (New York: Barnes and Noble, 1993), p. xiii.

Page 8 "the surviving emotional": *Hans Holzer's Haunted America*, p. xii.

Page 18 "lovingly, imploringly": *Phantom Encounters* by the Editors of Time-Life Books (Alexandria, VA: Time-Life, 1988), p. 23.

Page 19 "Back already?": *Best True Ghost Stories of the 20th Century* by David C. Knight (Englewood Cliffs, NJ: Prentice-Hall, 1984), p. 63.

Page 22 "Ladies, you will": *Atlas of the Supernatural* by Derek and Julia Parker (New York: Prentice Hall, 1990), p. 139.

Page 29 "vaguely mocking": *Phantom Encounters*, p. 98.

Page 30 "An art student" and "A man dressed": *Hauntings* by the Editors of Time-Life Books (Alexandria, VA: Time-Life, 1989), p. 129.

Page 36 "the best authenticated": *Unbidden Guests: A Book of Real Ghosts* by William Oliver Stevens (New York: Dodd, Mead, 1945), p. 52.

Page 37 "deaf and dumb": *Unbidden Guests*, p. 54.

Page 38 "By the Eternal": *Prominent American Ghosts* by Susy Smith (Cleveland: World, 1967), p. 109.

Page 41 "If poltergeist outbreaks": *Parapsychology: The Controversial Science* by Richard S. Broughton (New York: Ballantine, 1991), p. 231.

Page 51 "Some poltergeists are": *Hauntings*, p. 74.

Page 56 "large and handsome": *The Encyclopedia of Ghosts* by Daniel Cohen (New York: Dorset Press, 1984), p. 39.

Page 58 "I will not": *Prominent American Ghosts*, p. 6.

Page 61 "Sudden death": "Ghostbusters at Work" by Joyce and Richard Wolkomir, *McCall's*, July 1989, p. 106.

Page 67 "They usually give": "Ghostbusters at Work," p. 106.

# About the Author

Gary L. Blackwood is a novelist and playwright who specializes in historical topics. His interest in the Unexplained goes back to his childhood, when he heard his father tell a story about meeting a ghost on a lonely country road.

Though he has yet to see a single UFO or ghost, a glimpse of the future or a past life, the author is keeping his eyes and his mind open. Gary lives in Missouri with his wife and two children.